Rocket into Ricky's World

Respecting Siblings

By T. M. Merk

Published by The Child's World®
1980 Lookout Drive • Mankato, MN 56003-1705
800-599-READ • www.childsworld.com

Photographs: Celig/Shutterstock.com, cover, 1, 7, 9, 17; glenda/Shutterstock.com, 4; kwanchai.c/Shutterstock.com, 11; Mikhail Rulkov/Shutterstock.com, 13; Alrandir/Shutterstock.com, 15; Tomsickova Tatyana/Shutterstock.com, 19
Icons: © Aridha Prassetya/Dreamstime, 3, 7, 11, 13, 22

Copyright ©2019 by The Child's World®
All rights reserved. No part of this book may be reproduced or utilized in any form or by any means without written permission from the publisher.

ISBN HARDCOVER: 9781503827424
ISBN PAPERBACK: 9781622434442
LCCN: 2017961939

Printed in the United States of America
PA02379

About the Author

T.M. Merk is an elementary educator with a master's degree in elementary education from Lesley University in Cambridge, Massachusetts. Drawing on years of classroom experience, she enjoys creating engaging educational material that inspires students' passion for learning. She lives in New Hampshire with her husband and her dog, Finn.

Table of Contents

Rocket into Ricky's World ———— 5

Respectful Talk ———————————— 20

S.T.E.A.M. Activity ——————————— 21

Glossary ———————————————— 22

To Learn More ———————————— 23

Index ————————————————— 24

Rocket into Ricky's World

Ricky and his brother, Luke, loved to make things. When their dad gave them a big box, they wanted to turn it into a rocket ship!

"The rocket ship should be blue!" said Ricky.

"No, green," argued Luke.

"I'm older than you, so I'm the boss!" said Ricky.

You should treat other people the way that you want to be treated. Think about the things that make you feel happy. Do you like when your **sibling** shares his or her toys with you? What about when someone speaks to you in a kind way or helps you? If you want people to be nice, helpful, and respectful to you, you should be the same to them.

Leo the paintbrush waved his arms.

"Stop fighting!" he said. "Ricky and Luke, it's time to brush up on respect. You both have great ideas. Why don't you **compromise**?"

"What does compromise mean?" Ricky asked.

"When you compromise, you find a way to respectfully agree," Leo said. "You can use both ideas or a new idea."

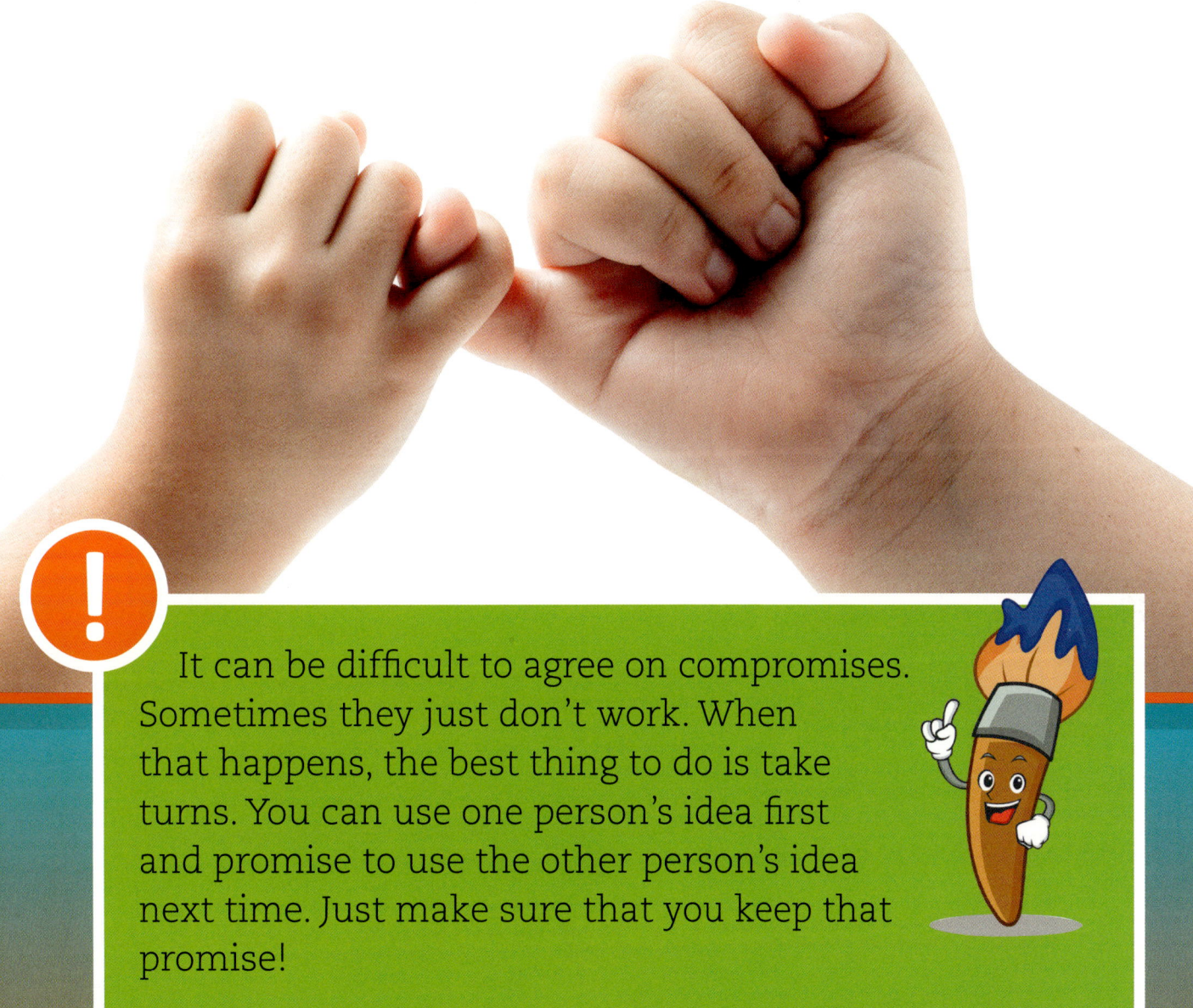

It can be difficult to agree on compromises. Sometimes they just don't work. When that happens, the best thing to do is take turns. You can use one person's idea first and promise to use the other person's idea next time. Just make sure that you keep that promise!

"I like that plan," Luke said, "but Ricky says he should be the boss because he's older."

Leo smiled. "Being siblings is more special than being older or younger. It means that you should care for each other, stand up for each other, and **encourage** each other. You should **respect** each other's ideas, space, and **belongings**."

! What does it mean to stand up for each other? Sometimes another person might be disrespectful to your sibling. If you see that happen, you should tell that person that he or she is being unkind. You can help your sibling if he or she is treated in a bad way.

"We do have a lot more fun when we're nice to each other," Ricky said. "I'm sorry, Luke. We can paint the rocket ship blue *and* green."

"Good idea!" Leo said.

"And maybe you can help me draw a cool robot on the side of the rocket ship, Ricky," Luke said.

"Sure! It's easy," Ricky said. "Pick out a good spot and we'll get to work."

Leo knew that the boys understood. Respecting each other is more important than getting your own way. Brothers (and sisters) have to stick together!

Respectful Talk

Do you need help talking in a respectful way to your sibling or siblings? Use these sentence starters to help!

- I have a great idea. We could ...
- I like your idea, but what about ...
- We could use both ideas because ...
- Maybe we could try that, or maybe we could try ...
- We can do _____ first, and then _____ after that.
- This time let's use my idea, but next time I promise that we can use yours!

S.T.E.A.M. Activity

Create an Airplane That Flies When You Throw It

Directions: Using only the materials provided, create an airplane that can travel a far distance. You may cut, tape, or color on any of the materials.

Time Constraints: You may use a total of 30 minutes for your creation. You are allowed 15 minutes to plan and 15 minutes to build your airplane. When you're done, take turns seeing how far your airplane can travel.

Discussion: Did you make sure each person was able to share his or her idea? Was anybody trying to be the boss? Did you find a way to compromise or a fair way to make a decision? What worked really well? What could you do better next time?

Suggested Materials:
- Construction paper
- Cardboard
- Cardstock
- Plastic straws
- Tape
- Glue
- Safety scissors
- Markers/crayons

Glossary

belongings: (buh-LONG-ings) Belongings are things that are yours. They are your property.

compromise: (KOM-pruh-myz) To compromise is to use a little bit of one person's idea and a little bit of another person's idea.

encourage: (en-KUR-ij) To encourage is to urge someone to do something or to cheer for someone.

respect: (rih-SPEKT) To respect is to show that you care about a person, place, thing, or idea.

sibling: (SIB-ling) Your sibling is your brother or sister.

To Learn More

Books

Child, Lauren. *I've Won, No I've Won, No I've Won.* New York, NY: Grosset & Dunlap, 2006.

Keats, Ezra Jack. *Peter's Chair.* New York, NY: Viking Books for Young Readers, 2006.

Pham, LeUyen. *Big Sister, Little Sister.* New York, NY: Hyperion Books for Children, 2005.

Web Sites

Visit our Web site for links about respecting siblings:
childsworld.com/links

Note to Parents, Teachers, and Librarians: We routinely verify our Web links to make sure they are safe and active sites. So encourage your readers to check them out!

Index

B
belongings, 12

C
compromise, 8, 10, 11

E
encourage, 12

R
respect, 7, 8, 12, 18

S
sibling, 7, 12, 13

standing up for each other, 13

T
taking turns, 11